The Adventures of Big Sil™ Los Angeles, CA

Written by A.J. Bennett
Illustrated by Drew Lewis
Photography by Wendy Smith

Copyright © 2016 by Big Sil LLC.
All rights reserved. No part of this publication may be reproduced, distributed, or transmitted in any form or by any means, including photocopying, recording, or other electronic or mechanical methods, without the prior written permission of Big Sil LLC.
For permission requests visit bigsilbooks.com.
THE ADVENTURES OF BIG SIL is a registered trademark of Big Sil LLC.
ISBN 978-0-9967352-2-3 Printed in the US.

Stuck inside on a rainy, grey day.

Little Ange and Big Sil imagine fun places to play.

Big Sil lands in warm, sunny LA.

Big Sil visits an observatory with a view.

Big Sil sees stars, at a show in the dark.

Big Sil sees a waterfall on a hike in Griffith Park.

In Hollywood there is more to explore.

At the movie makers,
Big Sil takes a studio tour.

Big Sil goes to the Farmers Market for fresh food.

Lots of healthy fruit,
puts him in a good mood.

One day, Big Sil will have a star to mark his name.

At the tar pits, black goo gurgles up slow.

There are fossils from 38,000 years ago.

Big Sil goes to an art museum on Gallery Row.

Big Sil tries surfing for the first time. Whoa!

Santa Monica Pier glows, as the sun starts to set.

Big Sil walks on the beach, but he never gets his paws wet!

www.ingramcontent.com/pod-product-compliance
Lightning Source LLC
Chambersburg PA
CBHW041127300426
44113CB00002B/83